Joke-Away and Riddles Plus

Compiled by Robert F. Vitarelli

Illustrations by Dulcianne Vye

Xerox Education Publications

Teacher: "Why is TV better than a radio?"
Pupil: "Not only can you hear the static, you can see it, too!"

Question: What does a farmer grow if he works very hard?
Answer: Tired!

Bill: "Why are hurricanes always named after girls?"
Jill: "Did you ever hear of a himmicane?"

Teacher: There will be an eclipse of the moon tonight. Perhaps your parents will let you stay up to watch it.

Pupil: What channel is it on?

Question: Why does a bear sleep through the winter?

Answer: Who's going to wake up a bear?

Question: How do you stop a bull from charging?

Answer: Take away his credit card.

How's Business?

Tailor: "Just sew-sew."

Farmer: "Mine is growing."

Author: "All write."

Astronomer: "It's looking up."

Trash Collector: "It's picking up."

Electrician: "It's pretty light."

Elevator Operator: "Mine has its ups and downs."

Question: What time is it when an elephant sits on a fence?
Answer: Time to get a new fence.

Question: What starts with a T, ends with a T, and is full of T?
Answer: A teapot.

Question: What did one candle say to the other candle?
Answer: These birthdays burn me up!

Question: What did one hot dog say to the other?
Answer: Hi, Frank!

Sally: "Why does an elephant wear green sneakers?"
Sue: "So he can hide in the grass!"

Question: What did the beaver say to the tree?
Answer: It's been nice gnawing you!

Question: What is more useful after it's broken?
Answer: An egg.

Mary: "Why did the man put his car in the oven?"
Larry: "He wanted a hot rod."

Question: If you throw a white stone into the Red Sea, what will it become?
Answer: Wet!

Daffynition:
  Indistinct: Where people put dirty dishes.

Tarzan: "What do you know when three elephants walk down the street wearing pink shirts?"
Jane: "They're all on the same team!"

Daffynitions:
  Knapsack: a sleeping bag
  Kindred: a fear of relatives
  Humbug: a person who loves to hum.

Jim: My brother fell off a 12-foot tree.
Kim: Did he get hurt?
Jim: No, he had only climbed up 2 feet.

Father: I wonder why that clock is so slow?
Know-It-All-Son: You would be slow, too, if you were running all day!

Question: What word is usually pronounced wrong by the best of scholars?
Answer: Wrong!

Hunter: I spotted a leopard!
Wife: Don't be silly, dear. They grow that way!

Question: What do they call tiny spotted cats in Florida?
Answer: Kittens!

Question: Why does a baby pig eat so much?
Answer: To make a pig of himself!

Knock, knock!
Who's there?
Dwain.
Dwain who?
Dwain the bathtub—I'm dwowning!

Question: What are people doing every day?
Answer: Growing older.

Daffynition: Tot's tricycle—a tot rod.

Mother: "Dear, would you like some more alphabet soup?"
Daughter: "I couldn't eat another syllable."

Sam: "How can you drop an egg four feet without breaking it?"
Tam: "I don't know. How?"
Sam: "Drop it five feet. The first four feet, it won't break."

11

Tim: "Did you ever see an elephant hide in a tree?"
Jim: "No."
Tim: "They hide pretty well, don't they!"

Jack: "Did your watch stop when it dropped on the floor?"
Mack: "Of course. Did you expect it to go right through?"

Waiter: "How did you find the steak, sir?"
Diner: "By accident. I moved the potatoes and there it was."

Question: What's the longest word in the English language?
Answer: SMILES—there's a mile between each S.

Frank: "How can you tell a dogwood tree?"
Mary Lou: "By its bark!"

Knock, knock.
Who's there?
Catsup.
Catsup who?
Catsup a tree!

Tim: "Why does Ted work as a baker?"
Jim: "I guess he kneads the dough."

Customer: "This coffee tastes like mud."
Waiter: "Well, it was ground this morning."

Question: What is the meaning of the word illegal?
Answer: A big, sick bird.

Gil: "Why can't a bike stand up on its own?"
Bill: "Because it's two-tired."

Father: "Look at all these bills! Rent, heat, clothes, food—the cost of living is going up on all of them. I'd be happy if just one thing went down."
Son: "Here's my report card, Dad!"

Customer: "Say, what is this in my soup?"
Waiter: "I can't say, sir. I don't know one insect from another."

Plane Passenger: "My, those people down there look like ants."
Neighbor: "They are ants. We haven't started flying yet."

Al: "What colors would you paint the sun and the wind?"
Sal: "The sun rose and the wind blue."

Andy: "I keep seeing spots before my eyes."
Oscar: "Have you seen a doctor?"
Andy: "No, just spots."

Question: Why did the farmer feed his cow money?
Answer: He wanted rich milk.

Have you ever seen: a board walk, a cow hide, a fish bowl, a horse fly, a barn dance, a fish fry, a corn stalk, an ocean wave, a door catch, a fire escape, a snow bank, a train trip, or a store sign?

Bill: "The brain is a wonderful thing."
Will: "Why do you say that?"
Bill: "The human brain starts working the moment you get up in the morning, and never stops until you're called on in class."

Bill: "What did Tennessee?"
Will: "The same thing Arkansas."

Sue: "What a nice dog. How long have you had him?"
Lou: "For years. He's like one of the family."
Sue: "Which one?"

Jill: "Do you have any trouble making decisions?"
Jane: "Well, yes and no."

Speeder: "Officer, was I driving too fast?"
Officer: "No, you were flying too low."

Rose: "My dog can do arithmetic."
Teacher: "He can?"
Rose: "I ask him how much two minus two is and he says nothing."

Question: If all of the cars in the U.S. were pink, what would we have?
Answer: A pink carnation.

Teacher: "What family does the walrus belong to?"
Pupil: "I don't know. No family near us has one."

Mrs. Jones: "Why are you knitting three socks?"
Mrs. Smith: "My son says he's grown another foot since he went in the army."

Harry: "I'm going to buy a farm two miles long and half an inch wide."
Larry: "What would you grow on a farm that size?"
Harry: "Spaghetti."

Ann: "What is yellow and wears a mask?"
Nan: "The Lone Lemon."

Ted: "Does your dog have a license?"
Ned: "No. He's not old enough to drive."

Customer: "I want a pancake, and please hurry up. Will it be long?"
Cook: "No, sir, it will be round."

Question: Where were the first doughnuts made?
Answer: In Greece.

Tim: "I haven't slept for days."
Jim: "Wow, you must be tired."
Tim: "Not really. I sleep nights."

Cowboy: "Just call me Tex."
Girl: "Are you from Texas?"
Cowboy: "No, I'm from Maryland, but I sure don't want to be called Mary!"

Two Hollywood goats found some old film and began to eat it.
"Is it good?" asked one.
"Yes, but I liked the book better," was the reply.

Father helping son in arithmetic: "If A made $75 and B spends $100—ask your mother to help you. This is right down her alley."

Policeman: "Here's a ticket for parking, lady."
Lady: "Oh, good! What time does it start?"

A woman telephoned an airline office in New York City and asked, "How long does it take to fly to San Francisco?" "Just a minute," said the man who answered. "Thank you," said the woman and she hung up.

Ted: "How can you spell mousetrap?"
Fred: "CAT!"

Teacher: "Joe, name the four seasons."
Joe: "Salt, pepper, vinegar, and mustard."

Lady: "Do you have hot and cold water in this hotel?"
Clerk: "Yes, ma'am. Cold in winter and hot in summer."

Joy: "If you put three ducks in a box, what would you have?"
Roy: "A box of quackers!"

Ron: "Why is a bad riddle like a poor pencil?"
Don: "Because it has no point."

Mary: "Why is a river rich?"
Jane: "Because it has two banks."

Doctor: "How's the man who swallowed the spoon?"
Nurse: "He can hardly stir."

John: "A man lost his dog in the woods and searched for the dog for hours. How did he find him again?"

Ron: "He listened to the bark all around him."

Question: How can you avoid getting that run-down feeling?

Answer: Look both ways before crossing the street!

Question: Why does a window squeak?

Answer: Because it has panes.

Bob: Can you name the four new states?

Fritz: But there are only two, Hawaii and Alaska.

Bob: No, there are four—New York, New Jersey, New Mexico, and New Hampshire!

Two boys standing at a railroad station.
First boy: "A train just passed."
Second boy: "How can you tell?"
First boy: "I can see its tracks."

Sue: "What did the jack say to the car?"
Ben: "Can I give you a lift?"

Tillie: "What is green and goes 'SLAM, SLAM, SLAM, SLAM'?"
Willie: "A four-door pickle."

New Invention: A fountain pen with a meatball point. It writes under gravy.

Reg: "How do you like your new chimney sweeping job?"
Bob: "It soots me!"

Jim: "What kind of train carries gum?"
Lyn: "A chew-chew train."

A woman who was driving along a country road saw two repairmen climbing a telephone pole.

"Look at them," she said. "They think I've never driven before."

Jay: "What was purple and conquered the world?"
Corey: "Alexander the Grape!"

Xavier: "Do you think you can catch my cold?"
Zeke: "I don't know. How fast does it run?"

Ron: "What did one tonsil say to the other?"
Don: "Get dressed. The doctor is taking us out tonight."

Customer: "When I bought this cat, you told me he was good for mice. He doesn't go near them."
Clerk: "Well, isn't that good for mice?"

Question: Why do bees hum?
Answer: Because they don't know the words.

First Grader: "We learned to say 'Yes, Sir' and 'No, Sir' today."
Father: "You did?"
First Grader: "Yeah!"

Clem: "What's smarter than a talking horse?"
Lem: "A spelling bee."

Question: Why does electricity shock people?
Answer: It doesn't know how to conduct itself.

New Invention: Fountain pen with butterball point. It writes on toast.

Mother: "Why are you taking so long to fill the saltshakers?"
Son: "It's hard getting the salt through these little holes!"

Fred: "Do you know how to play ball?"
Red: "Yes, of course."
Fred: "How do you hold a bat?"
Red: "By the wings!"

Alice: "What do you do when an elephant hurts its big toe?"
Bob: "Call a big tow truck."

Jack: "What did one washing machine say to the other?"
Jan: "I don't know."
Jack: "See you later, agitator."

Question: Why did the lady go outside with her purse open?
Answer: She expected a change in the weather!

O'Toole: "When does an Irish potato change its nationality?"
O'Boyle: "When it becomes French fries!"

Nancy: Why do birds fly north?
Betty: Because it's too far to walk!

Sally: "What is bought by the yard but worn by the foot?"
Kim: "A carpet!"

Jack: "Who first flew at Kitty Hawk? Was it Orville or Wilbur?"
Jill: "I don't know, but either one is Wright!"

Bill: "Why don't many elephants go to college?"
George: "Because not very many are graduated from high school!"

Question: How do you make a car top?
Answer: Tep on the brake, tupid!

The laziest man I knew was Will Knot. Instead of writing his name he just wrote **Won't**!

Peg: "Do you believe in free speech?"
Meg: "Sure I do!"
Peg: "Then may I use your phone?"

Question: What runs around the farmyard yet never moves?
Answer: The fence.

Question: What is hard and flat, thin and round, when its head is up and tail is down?
Answer: A coin.

Swimmer: "Are you sure there are no crocodiles at this beach?"
Lifeguard: "Quite sure. The sharks chase them away!"

Moe: "What would you get if you crossed a potato with an onion?"
Joe: "A spud with watery eyes!"

Teen: "Why don't you do the jerk?"
Dad: "My go-go is gone-gone!"

Question: Where do old Volkswagens go?
Answer: To the **Old Volks** home.

He: "Did you hear the rope joke?"
She: "No, skip it!"

Pal: "Were you in the boat when it tipped over?"
Sal: "No, silly, I was in the water!"

34

Terry: "What would you do if you were in my shoes?"

Jerry: "I'd polish them."

Son: "Dad, there was a man here to see you."

Dad: "With a bill?"

Son: "No. His nose was just like yours."

Joe: "If buttercups are yellow, what color are hiccups?"

Moe: "Burple!"

Earl: "My dog started chewing up the dictionary."

Pearl: "What did you do?"

Earl: "I took the words right out of his mouth."

Lady in Street: "Officer, how can I get to the hospital?"

Officer: "Just stand where you are."

Mary: "Did you hear about the guy with the gleam in his teeth?"

Paul: "Yes, he was bumped while he was brushing his teeth."

Ed: "That's a strange pair of socks you have on —one red and the other green."

Fred: "Yes, and the funny thing about it is that I have another pair at home exactly like this one."

Sam: "Excuse me. I think you are sitting in my seat."

Bully: "Can you prove it?"

Sam: "I think so. I left my pie and ice cream on it!"

Question: What did the leopard say after he ate the hot dog?
Answer: That just hit the spot.

Question: What did one math book say to the other?
Answer: I've got problems!

Question: What gets lost every time you stand up?
Answer: Your lap.

Mother: "Eddie, don't be selfish. Let your little brother have the sled half the time."
Eddie: "I do. I have it going down and he has it going up."

Herb: "Last night I stayed up all night trying to find out where the sun goes after it goes down."
Jack: "Did you find out?"
Herb: "Yes. It finally dawned on me!"

High School Boy: "Are you the barber who cut my hair the last time?"
Barber: "I couldn't be. I've only been here for three months."

Boss: "Where's my pencil?"
Helper: "Behind your ear."
Boss: "Come, come, I'm a busy man. Which ear?"

Jim: "What did Benjamin Franklin say when he discovered electricity?"
Tim: "Nothing, he was too shocked."

Ann: "When is a piece of wood like a king or a queen?"
Nan: "When it's a ruler."

Lem: "What' kind of shoes are made from banana skins?"
Clem: "Slippers!"

Barber: "Your hair seems to be turning grey."
Customer: "I'm not surprised. Can't you work a little faster?"

Sammy: "Do you think that anyone can tell the future with cards?"

Danny: "My mother can. She takes a look at my report card and then tells me exactly what will happen when my father gets home."

Daffynitions:
Mischief: The chief's daughter.
Banana split: An acrobatic fruit.

Boy: "When I sat down to play the piano, every-one laughed at me."
Mother: "For goodness sakes! Why?"
Boy: "No piano bench!"

Flo: "What's big and red and doesn't eat rocks?"
Joe: "A big, red rock eater on a diet!"

Quizmaster: "How many successful jumps must a paratrooper make before he graduates?"
Contestant: "All of them."

Jed: "What is a raisin?"
Ned: "A worried grape."

Joan: "Which burns longer, a red or a green candle?"

George: "Neither one. Both of them burn shorter."

Lady: "I want a ticket to Chicago."

Ticket Agent: "Yes, ma'am. Would you like to go by Buffalo?"

Lady: "Of course not! I want to go by train."

Rena: "How do you drive a baby buggy, Alan?"
Alan: "Tickle its toes."

Customer: "Give me a hot dog, please."
Cook: "With pleasure!"
Customer: "No thanks, with mustard."

Paul: "Where is the English Channel?"
Paula: "I don't know. Our TV set only gets American channels."

Sister: "Did you take a bath?"
Brother: "Why? Is there one missing?"

Joe: "Please give me a bottle of acetylsalicylic acid."
Druggist: "You mean aspirin?"
Joe: "That's it! I can never remember that name!"

Doug: "What's the best way to catch a squirrel?"
Lorrie: "Just climb a tree and act like a nut!"

Bob: "May I hold your hand?"
Pam: "No thanks, it's not heavy."

Ed: "What is long, green, slimy, and very dangerous?"
Ted: "A thundering herd of pickles."

Dan: "If Mississippi gave Missouri her New Jersey, what would Delaware?"
Jan: "I don't know, but Alaska!"

Sal: "Have you heard the one about the mountain?"
Bev: "Yeah, it's just a big bluff!"

Boy: "Mom, I can't."
Mother: "Son, never say you can't do something. Nothing is impossible if you really try!"
Boy: "OK, Mom, then please help me put the toothpaste back in the tube!"

Sherry: "Why do ducks have flat feet?"
Roy: "Gosh, I don't know."
Sherry: "To put out forest fires! And why do elephants have flat feet?"
Roy: "Why?"
Sherry: "To put out flaming ducks!"

Harry: "Gee, that policeman's strong!"
Gary: "I'll say. He can hold up hundreds of cars with one hand!"

Roy: "Did you hear about the angel who lost his job?"
Joy: "What happened?"
Roy: "He had harp failure!"

Doctor: "Nobody lives forever."
Patient: "Mind if I try?"

Peg: "What time is it?"
Meg: "I don't know."
Peg: "Well, what does your watch say?"
Meg: "Tick-tock, tick-tock!"

Fred: "How many sides does a circle have?"
Red: "Two. An inside and an outside."

Jake: "When the clock strikes 13, what time is it?"
Sol: "Time to get a new clock!"

Farmer: "I put fertilizer and water on my strawberries. What do you put on yours?"
City Boy: "Milk and sugar."

Teacher: "Let's talk about grizzly bears. Do we get fur from them?"
Boy: "I get as **fur** away from them as I can!"

Nellie: "How did the octopus go into battle?"
Howie: "Well-armed."

Mother: "Eat your spinach, it puts color in your cheeks."
Little Girl: "Who wants green cheeks?"

First Mosquito: "Why are you limping?"
Second Mosquito: "I came through the screen door and strained myself."

Liz: "What's a comet?"
Diz: "A star with a tail."
Liz: "Can you give me an example?"
Diz: "Lassie."

Customer: "Do you serve crabs?"
Waiter: "Yes, we serve anyone, sir."

A: "What do spooks call their army?"
B: "The Ghost Guard."

Jane: "What model is your car?"
Jill: "It's not a model, it's a horrible example."

Boy: "Why is that elephant lying on its back?"
Girl: "So it can trip the birds."

Prue: "Boy, is my cat smart!"
Sue: "Why?"
Prue: "It eats cheese and then stands by the mousehole with baited breath."

Neil: "This match won't light."
Mark: "What's the matter with it?"
Neil: "I don't know. It worked all right before."

Joe: "What has 43 teeth, 5 feet, 10 hands, and breathes fire?"

Moe: "I don't know. But whatever it is, you'd better run if you ever see it coming."

Boy: "Mom, may I have a puppy for my birthday this year?"

Mother: "Well, dear, they cost ten dollars apiece."

Boy: "Yes, but I want a whole one."

Fritz: "Why does a dog turn around twice before it lies down?"

Janet: "Because one good turn deserves another."

Question: Why did the man put the radio in the refrigerator?
Answer: He wanted to hear cool music.

Smarty: "I have something hard to beat."
Alec: "What's that?"
Smarty: "A hard-boiled egg!"

Lynn: "Why are famous baseball players always cool at games?"
Margo: "Because they have fans in the stands."

Sandy: "Why did you get zero on your spelling paper?"
Ian: "That's not a zero. The teacher ran out of stars so she gave me a moon."

Cathy: "Did your father fly from Ohio?"
Fred: "Yes, and are his arms tired!"

Toni: "Did you hear about the fight in the candy store?"
Libbi: "No, what happened?"
Toni: "Two suckers got licked."

Bob: "What would it be like to have eight arms?"
Mary Lou: "Very handy!"

Teddy: "I went riding this morning."
Betty: "Horseback?"
Teddy: "Oh, yes. He got back two hours before I did!"

Dick: "Is there much difference between the North Pole and the South Pole?"
Nick: "All of the difference in the world."

Bill: "What is purple and skims over the water?"
Phil: "An outboard grape."

Question: What did one ghost say to the other ghost?
Answer: Don't spook until spooken to!

Question: What is the best way to get a rug out from under an elephant?
Answer: Wait until he leaves.

Girl: "May I have ten cents for a man who is crying outside?"
Mom: "The poor man. What is he crying about?"
Girl: "Ice cream—ten cents!"

Wise Guy: "I'd like a round trip ticket to the moon."
Clever Ticket Agent: "Sorry, sir, the moon is full right now."

Customer: "Is there any soup on the menu?"
Waiter: "There was, but I wiped it off."

Question: What is the best thing to put into a piece of pie?
Answer: Your teeth!

Steve: "I just found a horseshoe."
Dave: "Do you know what that means?"
Steve: "Yeah. It means that some poor horse is running around in his stocking feet!"

Country: "Just think of our forest preserves."
City: "And our subway jams."

Nancy: "What goes through the woods without making a sound?"
Ellen: "A path."

Cathy: "What did the clock's big hand say as it left the little hand?"
Jon: "I don't know. What?"
Cathy: "See you in an hour."

Harry: "When was beef the highest?"
Larry: "When the cow jumped over the moon!"

Lady: "Why did that man put on a wet shirt?"
Gentleman: "Because it said wash and wear."

Airplane: "I'll get the fishing poles and you get the bait."
Helicopter: "Why do I have to get the bait?"
Airplane: "Everybody knows that the whirly-bird gets the worm."

Monster: "I have a bad pain in my head."
Doctor: "Which head?"

Salesman: "Wow! Did I get two orders today!"
Boss: "That's great! What are they?"
Salesman: "Stay out and keep out!"

Question: What happens when a duck flies upside down?
Answer: He quacks up!

Question: What animal has its eyes closest together?
Answer: The smallest!